Get the Grant:
Your No B.S. Introduction to Foundation Grants

Get the Grant:
Your No B.S. Introduction to Foundation Grants

FIRST EDITION

By Ashley Cain and Bruce Ripley

CINCINNATI, OH

Copyright © 2019 by Painted Post Publications
Ashley Cain & Bruce Ripley

All rights reserved
Printed in the United States of America

No part of this book may be reproduced in any manner whatsoever without written permission except in the case of brief quotations embodied in articles, essays, blog posts, and reviews. Information and requests may be sent to:
Painted Post Publications
3414 Millikin Rd. Fairfield Twp., OH 45011

ISBN: 9781795354707

Contents

Introduction	Pg. 6
Chapter 1: Why Seek Foundation Grants for Your Nonprofit Organization?	Pg. 10
Chapter 2: What You Need Before Applying for Grants	Pg. 16
Chapter 3: Program Design & Evaluation	Pg. 28
Chapter 4: Diversity on Multiple Fronts	Pg. 39
Chapter 5: A Note to New Nonprofits (and To Those Thinking About Starting One)	Pg. 43
Chapter 6: How to Find Foundations Who May Support Your Mission	Pg. 48
Chapter 7: The Nuts & Bolts of Grant Writing	Pg. 53
Chapter 8: General Writing Tips	Pg. 77
Chapter 9: Cultivating Relationships with Grant Makers	Pg. 80
Chapter 10: The Ethics of Grant Writing	Pg. 90
Chapter 11: When You Should Hire a Freelancer, a Staff Grant Writer, or DIY	Pg. 98
In Closing	Pg. 101
Appendix	Pg. 102

About the Authors   Pg. 104

Introduction

Once in a while, when he's in the area on business, Bruce drives through seedy parts of Covington, Kentucky.

Don't worry, he's not looking to score drugs. He just occasionally likes to see the tangible evidence of his grant writing efforts.

He doesn't have to drive far in any direction to see it. Near the Licking River, Bruce spots the apartment building housing eleven formerly homeless men and women rejoining the community from which they had been isolated. Bruce's writing raised several million dollars for this organization's housing program over a period of many years.

Several blocks away sits the large white building that once housed a residential addiction treatment program for women. It was the only such program in Northern Kentucky that allowed women to bring their children with them to treatment. Previously, they would have to give up custody of their children…or simply pass on getting help.

Ashley has experienced something like this, too. She can see the impact of her work in programs for children and seniors at her local community arts center. Those programs once struggled, but are now thriving and changing lives. Her work is also evident in the ever-increasing number of students joining a regional youth symphony for which she secured millions in grant awards over the years.

Ashley's work has largely focused on arts organizations. Sometimes, the arts are a hard sell. Especially during lean years, like those the country experienced during the "Great Recession" of the late 2000s. Regardless, her belief in the power of the arts to change lives for the better has driven her work to help arts nonprofits win grant awards, even when making the case is difficult.

Herein lies the beauty of grant writing.

As a direct result of our writing, programs benefiting the community get implemented. People addicted to heroin get treatment. Children who might not otherwise hear a symphony perform get to do so.

Bruce and Ashley get the satisfaction of making this happen while making a decent living. Starving writers we are not!

Why have we written this book? Simply, we want to shorten less experienced grant writers' learning curves by walking you through what we learned through trial and error. A lot of trial and error.

When Bruce entered grant writing, there was no professional association chapter in Cincinnati specifically for grant writers. The internet was not the fountain of information that it is now.

He learned the art and science of grant writing by reading old proposals collecting dust in his office and piecing together bits of advice from multiple people. He also studied his junk mail. Why? Because in direct mail, every word counts.

Similarly, Ashley learned grant writing from nonprofit mentors who had no choice but to learn how to do it, since there weren't enough staff at their organizations to do it all. She spent hours poring over old grant files, learning why some proposals succeeded while others were rejected.

Today, Cincinnati has a Grant Professionals Association chapter (of which Ashley and Bruce are members) and everyone has access to the vast world wide web.

Yet, it can be hard to synthesize all of that information. We pull it all together for you here.

Plus, despite all of the freely available information, some people still develop unrealistic expectations about grants and what they can do for their organizations. We are often contacted by new nonprofits who believe their odds of getting grants are far better than they actually are. This is one reason why we have devoted a chapter to new nonprofits and to people thinking about founding one.

Government grants can be a great way to support your programs. However, we are focusing on foundation grants because a number of nonprofits, particularly small nonprofits, are not realistic candidates to handle government grants and their associated requirements.

Foundation grant proposals require work, too. However, foundation grant reporting and evaluation requirements are usually less onerous than government grants, and many smaller nonprofits can reasonably pursue them, provided they follow the advice in this book.

In the next chapter, we reveal more about why your organization should pursue foundation grants.

Chapter 1:
Why Seek Foundation Grants for Your Nonprofit Organization?

Before we dive into this chapter, let's start with a few quick grant definitions:

<u>Grant:</u> Occasionally, we come across folks who do not understand what a grant even is. Briefly, a grant is a financial award given by a private or public organization to another organization (typically, but not always a nonprofit) in order to accomplish a specific purpose or goal.

<u>Federal grants</u>: These are grants issued by various federal government agencies (such as the National Institute of Health, the National Parks Service, the National Endowment for the Arts, etc.). The funds come from federal revenue that has been allocated for specific purposes and often as a result of legislation. Organizations apply directly to the federal government for some federal grants. In other cases, the federal government awards grants to the states who, in turn, distribute those funds to the local level via formula distributions or competitive grant processes. When federal funds are distributed in this fashion, they are commonly called "pass-through" grants.

State, local, or municipal grants are funded, administered and awarded by the state, city, or municipal government to which they are attached.

Foundation grants: These are grant awards given by non-government trusts or charitable corporations to nonprofit organizations which align with that foundation's goals and interests.
Foundations are typically formed by families looking for a way to invest or preserve their wealth, or for a way to honor the wishes and interests of a now-deceased family member. Other times, foundations are the charitable arm of a company, such as a regional bank.

Foundations usually have at least one stated funding priority, but often have several areas of interest. These interests guide the Foundation's board members in choosing which nonprofits and which programs will receive grant funding. For example, if a foundation states that they want to support nonprofit programs benefiting children undergoing cancer treatment, then nonprofits in the animal welfare sector need not apply.

With that out of the way, let's examine the question of why you would want to pursue foundation grants before or instead of the other types.

This book could easily have focused on state or federal grants, or even given a broad overview of seeking *all* the various types of grants available. Instead, we have chosen to focus just on foundation-level grants as these are the type of grant which *we* recommend nonprofits new to grant writing (or new in general) go after first.

Assuming you follow advice like ours, foundation grants frequently have a better return on investment, in terms of a grant writer's time versus the amount of grant dollars they can potentially secure. Because foundation-level grants are usually run by individuals or corporations, they seldom have the red tape and lengthy list of requirements that government grants entail. Some foundations do require a disproportionate amount of work relative to the potential grant amount, but this tends to be the exception rather than the rule. This has several advantages for would-be grant seekers.

For one thing, a nonprofit seeking a foundation grant may not require the lengthy track record of proven success that a federal or state grant may require. Even if you are applying for a government grant to start a new program, you often need a strong overall organizational track record and qualified staff already on board to be a realistic candidate. Some foundations, though certainly not all, are willing to give "seed money" to new programs and, occasionally, to newer organizations.

Here is another reason why foundation grants are a great first foray into the world of grants: they force nonprofits to think through program design, delivery, and evaluation. Ideally, nonprofits should put a lot of effort up front into determining how a program will be run, what defines success for that program, and how they will measure that success. However, that isn't always the case. Organizations in a hurry to bring their program to the community sometimes by-pass crucial planning elements.

Because most foundation grant makers require nonprofits to outline details about how the program will operate and be evaluated, these grants can become a good motivator for organizations to do this hard, necessary work.

Federal and state government grant applications vary in terms of how long they need to be and how long they take to complete, but they generally require a lot of work. If you get a government grant, your organization may have to spend a lot of time making sure you are in compliance with the grant terms. Government grants may require a lot more data collection and follow-up report details than a typical foundation grant. Foundation grants proposals can also vary widely in terms of the length of time and effort required to prepare them. However, they run a much wider gamut. Some foundations (usually smaller family foundations) require no more than a 1-2 page letter and may specifically limit your page, word or character counts. At the other end of the continuum, some foundations (for example, large foundations who give across the U.S) may require almost as much work as a government grant and impose quite a few requirements. A substantial number of foundations fall somewhere between these two extremes, but normally are less onerous than most government grant opportunities.

Another sound reason for pursuing foundation grants is for the social proof it provides for your organization. When you can point to a list of foundations which have made awards to your program, it signals to other grant makers, donors, and the community that your organization is a good investment. This can potentially lead to more funds coming in the door. At least in our region, foundation staff members often talk to people at other local foundations. If one foundation deems your organization to be a sound investment, chances are other foundations in your area will hear about it.

Lastly, foundation grant proposals can serve more than one purpose, and we all know nonprofits need to be masters of multi-tasking. Since they are less technical, shorter documents and are written in a more accessible style, they can easily pull double duty as an "elevator pitch" for your program. The content written for a foundation proposal can be repurposed for fundraising letters, website content, marketing materials, and a variety of other vehicles which introduce your program to various constituents.

And of course, proposals written for foundations can also give your organization somewhere to start when it *is* ready to write a government grant proposal. This way, you aren't stuck reinventing the wheel or writing something from scratch. Because, as any veteran writer can tell you, staring at a computer screen with nothing to start from usually leads to lots of frustration and (say it ain't so) procrastination.

Chapter 2:
What You Need Before Applying for Grants

To realistically apply for grants, you need to have the following documents on hand. Some of these documents, such as proof of your nonprofit status, will be submitted with almost every grant application you do. Other documents, such as your strategic plan, will seldom be submitted with your grant applications, but you need them on hand for both grant application and other purposes.

<u>Proof of 501(c)(3) status from the IRS.</u> If you do not have a letter from the IRS certifying your status as a 501(c)(3) nonprofit organization, forget about applying for grants. You must have this letter. Unless the funder prohibits you from attaching documents of any kind to your application, you should submit this with your grant application to assure the funder you are indeed a 501(c)(3) nonprofit.

<u>Board roster</u>. You should always submit a list of your organization's board members with your grant proposals, unless the funder's requirements preclude you from doing so.

Your board roster is arguably one of the most important documents you will submit with your grant proposals. Funders understandably want to know who is in charge of your organization and what expertise they bring to the table. Plus, it may help if someone reading your grant proposal knows one or more of your board members. Or, it may hurt (Bruce once googled the name of a client's board member and learned she had been sanctioned by a professional licensing board). In addition to listing names, you should also list each board member's occupation and place of business.

What if your organization maintains an advisory board? Unless you know the names or affiliations of one or more advisory board members will resonate with the funder, we advise against submitting your advisory board roster with grant proposals. Normally, funders mainly want to know who directly controls the fate of your organization. Your board of directors or board of trustees falls in this category. Your advisory board may influence your organization, but cannot make binding decisions like voting board members do.

What if there is a separate, but closely affiliated nonprofit whose sole purpose is to raise funds and/or manage an endowment on your organization's behalf? We advise against submitting this roster with your grant proposals because the affiliated nonprofit is not the grant applicant. Keep it simple and just submit a roster of voting board members from you, the applicant organization.

Most recent audit. In rare cases, a foundation may require you to submit your last two or three financial audits. Otherwise, foundations who require you to submit your audit normally just want your most recent one. Audits are expensive, especially if an organization receives a lot of federal government grants. However, they are essential for showing funders your organization is financially viable. If an audit reveals your organization's finances are a wreck, then you have problems a grant will not fix anyway.

IRS Form 990. The Form 990 is the Internal Revenue Service's main tool for gathering information about nonprofit organizations. Some foundations require you to submit your organization's Form 990 with grant requests. Do not submit your Form 990 unless the funders requests it. It is a public document. Anyone, including prospective funders, can set up a free account on Guidestar and view your Form 990 at no cost to them.

If your organization is not required by the IRS to file an IRS Form 990, you will definitely need some other viable proof of your organization's financial health, such as an audit.

Employer ID Number (EIN), also known as the Federal Employer Identification Number (FEIN). This is your unique 9-digit number assigned by the IRS to business entities operating in the United States. This number is shown in your proof of nonprofit status from the IRS. However, some grant application forms ask applicants to list it on the cover page.

<u>The current fiscal year organizational budget and the previous fiscal year's income and expense statement.</u> The organizational budget prepared by your finance department may or may not be suitable for submission with a grant proposal. Unless the funder's requirements leave you no choice but to submit a multiple-page budget, the organizational budget you use for grant proposal purposes should be one page.

Also, many organizations prepare internal budgets with acronyms or terms that may not make sense to an outsider. This is an additional reason why you should prepare a 1-page budget with line item names that anyone can understand.

If guidelines permit, you should also include a short narrative along with your budget or income & expense statement if one or more of the following conditions are present:

- There is a significant deviation in a particular income or expense line item from one year to the next. Why do you expect to generate 20% more revenue from Medicaid this year compared to last year? Why are you projecting a 25% drop in your personnel expenses? What are reasons why your organization had a deficit last year? Why are you projecting a deficit this year? Assume the funder has someone with a strong financial background who is reading your grant proposal, because this is usually the case.

- You are projecting a significant surplus or a significant deficit. Having one or the other does not mean you are a poor candidate for a grant. If a new, large project you're beginning is the cause, provide a simple explanation to this effect. A large surplus or deficit is more likely to be a problem if your organization has been incurring them for several consecutive years.

- You are projecting a significant increase or decrease in your budget from last year to this year. This could occur for innocuous reasons (starting a new but expensive program) or for reasons the funder may find troublesome (you lost a major revenue source). No matter what the reason is, explain it in simple terms and do not try to hide anything you would want to know if you were the funder. If you were rich, would you want to invest $50,000 in a business that is seriously considering shutting its doors in two years? Of course not. Foundations do not want to invest in similarly troubled nonprofits or programs either. If your organization or an individual program of yours is in that much trouble, you have a problem a grant will not fix anyway, so don't waste your time or theirs.

Income & expense statements. The income and expense statements you use for grant application purposes should not exceed one page. To get an idea of what line items are most appropriate for a foundation grant request, you can find examples using Google search terms such as "common grant application budget format" or "grant application budget form." The exact line items you include in your income and expense statement will vary somewhat according to you what your sources of revenue are, the general nature of your organization, and so on. Generally, depending on which line items are applicable to your organization, examples of revenue line items may include, but not necessarily be limited to the following:

- Donations;
- Special event proceeds;
- Foundation and corporate grants;
- Government grants;
- Government contracts/per diems;
- Program fees;
- United Way or other federated campaign proceeds;
- Membership dues;
- Admissions;
- Sales; and/or
- Rental income

Examples of possible expense line items include, but are not necessarily limited to the following:

- Salaries;
- Employee benefits and taxes;
- Professional fees (outside attorneys, accountants, and so on used by your organization);
- Equipment;
- Supplies;
- Telephone;
- Occupancy (utilities, maintenance, security, and other costs associated with occupying a building space);
- Insurance;
- Staff training and/or conferences;
- Travel;
- Bad debt expense (losses experienced by the organization because it sold goods or services without receiving immediate payments); and/or
- Depreciation

Program/project budgets: Your program budget will probably have many, or all of the same line items as those listed above for income and expense statements. However, budgets for, say, a renovation project will contain only those line items that are relevant to the renovations. When writing a budget for a time-limited project such as renovations or new construction, be sure your personnel expense line item reflects the estimated amount of time your existing staff members will spend on the project.

A short narrative may be necessary here if something is likely to raise questions from the person reviewing your request. For example, if your organization budget shows you project raising $250,000 from special events, but your program budget shows nothing for special event proceeds, briefly explain why. Are special event proceeds needed to support other programs that do not directly generate revenue? Does your finance staff make ultra-conservative projections for special event proceeds? Just look at your program budget (plus your organization-level financial documents), see if you spot anything that an outsider might raise questions about, and then answer accordingly.

Strategic plan: Applicants do not normally need to submit a copy of their organization's strategic plan with grant applications. However, it helps your case for support if you can honestly say your organization has a current strategic plan that has been approved by your board of directors.

Plus, where appropriate, you can briefly mention relevant portions of the strategic plan in your proposal narrative. Writing something like "Organization ABC is requesting a $100,000 challenge grant to purchase a high-impact technology phone system that strengthens our infrastructure, a key goal in Organization ABC's new strategic plan" is a stronger description than saying "Organization ABC needs a new telephone system."

At minimum, your organization's strategic plan should cover a 3-year period, but probably not longer than 5 years, due to how hard it is to forecast much farther than 5 years into the future.

Organizational chart: In our experience, most foundations do not request organizational charts as an attachment to grant proposals. However, some do. You're far better off having one prepared and on hand rather than scrambling to create one at the last minute.

Key staff information: Some grant proposals require information about key staff members of your organization. Some funders will specify who they regard as key staff. In other cases, the funder will let you identify your key staff members. At minimum, you should have 2-4 sentence bios describing the qualifications and experience of your organization's chief executive officer, chief operating officer, chief fundraiser, and chief financial officer, or the closest equivalent of any of these positions within your organization. If your organization has no or few paid staff, you can prepare bios about the experience and qualifications of your board officers.

Mission statement: Include your mission statement (which, ideally, is no more than one sentence) in every grant proposal you write, whether or not the funder specifically asks for it. Your mission statement is how you convey, very succinctly, who you are and what your organization is about. Make it count. Omitting your mission statement from your grant proposals is almost as bad as having a boring mission statement.

Organization history: Unless you are faced with severe space limits, include at least a few sentences about your organization's history in every grant request. Why was your organization founded? What needs were your founders attempting to address. If you can honestly say your organization was the first in your city, region, or state to start a specific type of program, feel free to mention it. Your history can also mention details such as major past expansions of your organization, if applicable, and any honors (preferably in recent years) your organization has received.

Your unique selling proposition (USP): Why does your organization pass the "who cares" test? How is your organization different from other organizations providing the same or similar services? Why should a foundation fund your organization instead one of the 173 other organizations who applied? You need to be able to spell out, in writing, why a funder ought to care about your organization. Like it or not, you are in the sales business when you write a grant proposal. You don't sell your organization quite the same way you would a car. However, assuming that funders will automatically recognize the awesomeness of your organization is a recipe for failure. Your individual programs may each need their own USP, because some programs may interest a particular funder while others do not.

Letters of support or testimonials: On rare occasions, a foundation may require you to obtain a letter of support from another nonprofit organization with whom you are collaborating, or who is familiar with your organization's work. Testimonials from satisfied clients or patrons can help your case. Ideally, you should use testimonials sent directly to you by someone who is happy with your organization's work. If you use positive comments found social media or online forums, you should note that in your proposal. Do not attach actual letters to applications unless requested to do so, or the funder allows you to attach/upload relevant attachments of your choosing.

Recent newspaper articles or other publicity: If allowed to attach them to your grant request, recent media coverage is hard to beat in terms of third party verification of your effectiveness.

Demographics and data about your target population: Your community has a high rate of poverty? How do you know? Saying in a grant proposal that your community has a high rate of poverty is not enough. You need hard numbers showing demographics about the target population within the community, region, census tract, or other geographic entity of interest to you and prospective funders. You should also maintain demographics and other relevant data about your organization's clients, patients, patrons, etc.

Board meeting minutes: These are private, internal documents that you should never send with a grant proposal. However, once in a great while, a foundation will require your board's approval in order to consider your grant request. Your board meeting minutes should reflect the vote and the results of that vote in such cases.

Articles of incorporation and bylaws: Foundations seldom require copies of these, but you should have them on hand anyway.

Chapter 3:
Program Design and Evaluation

First thing's first. Before we dive into this chapter, I'm going to give you some definitions that will be helpful in reading this chapter. If you are newer to the field of grant writing, this may be the first time you've seen some of these terms, but it definitely won't be the last.

Logic Model
Logic models are visual representations of your program. They can either show a cause and effect style flow of how a problem is addressed by a program or they may show a visual of all the moving pieces of the program in a way that helps you organize the grant proposal itself. Examples of both types are included in the appendix of this book.

Program Design
This is basically what it sounds like. Program design is how you create and mold a program to address a specified need and achieve desired goals and outcomes (more on these later in this chapter). Ideally, program designs should be based on best practices or successful models.

Program Evaluation

A systematic procedure for collecting and analyzing both qualitative and quantitative data about your program. This data is then used to determine the program's success in achieving stated goals, objectives, & outcomes.

Best Practices
A procedure or method that has been shown over time to produce the best results. In the nonprofit world, best practices are often identified as such after organizations run successful programs for many years and have collected data to proven and support their success.

Ok, let's move on to the good stuff.

Thinking through program design and evaluation is probably the most important thing you will do in the course of preparing to write a grant. Bold words, right? But we believe them and often, these are also the elements which get the least attention.

Let's face it. Thinking through logic models, program delivery, and methods of data collection are not the most riveting topics, but allow us to convince you of their merits and give you some easy ways to incorporate them into your grants process.

First and foremost, if you want to achieve a certain goal (obtaining grant awards) then it's often wise to begin with the end in mind. This means doing all of your planning upfront as if getting that grant is a foregone conclusion rather than writing a proposal on a hope and a prayer with the intention of fleshing out details later *if* you get the award. That last approach almost always leads to not delivering what you said you would. Besides, grant makers can usually smell your lack of preparation a mile away.

Grant makers want to know that your nonprofit's program is a wise investment and the best way to persuade them of that is to show that you have thought through every detail of how that program will function, what it will achieve and how, and how you will evaluate and report on its successes and challenges.

To get started, ask yourself these preliminary questions:

1. What would a grant maker need to know about my program in order to think it's worthwhile to fund it?
2. What would prove to the grant maker that the *need* exists for this program? For example, if the funder wants to have an impact on child poverty, how will you show your program reduces child poverty in your region?
3. What, specifically, do we want this program to achieve? What are the goals? How will we realistically get there?
4. How much money do we need to achieve the aims of the program? What other resources, if any, are needed (including staff)?

5. What would prove to this grant maker that my organization is the best one suited to *carry out* this program and achieve results?
6. How will we pull data out of the program to show the results of our work? What *types* of data will be most useful to evaluating our success?

With these questions in mind, there are a few ways you can organize your thoughts into a coherent program design which can ultimately lead to a well-written grant proposal. You can use a logic model (see examples), which is Ashley's favorite tool for this purpose. To help you understand the logic model and evaluate your programs, we should make sure you know what a few key terms mean:

Goal: What you ultimately want to accomplish. Bruce listed the following as a goal in a logic model required by the funder – "To improve the health of persons with substance use disorders participating in Northern Kentucky Drug Court by providing employment-focused recovery services." Notice how this describes what your ultimate aim is ("improve the health"), who this ultimate aim pertains to (persons with substance use disorders participating in Northern Kentucky Drug Court) and the mechanism for the ultimate aim (employment focused recovery services).

Objective: This is an action you take to help you accomplish the goal. In this instance, Bruce listed 3 broad objectives:

- Establish the infrastructure and processes of an integral employment program.
- To provide employment focused recovery reentry services to 175 persons over a 3 year period referred through Northern Kentucky Drug Court.
- To identify and secure continued funding for the project through viable sources.

Outcome: This is the measurable change observed in the people served as a result of your program. In this instance, Bruce listed 3 desired, quantifiable outcomes:

- 90% of persons will maintain reduced use of alcohol and other drugs at 6 months post treatment
- 50% of persons will maintain employment 6 months after completing program
- 75% of persons will not incur any new criminal convictions prior to program completion

When you work in an organization focused on the arts, culture, or humanities, creating goals, objectives, and outcomes can at times feel difficult. After all, so much of the value you provide is likely intangible, right? But now more than ever, these types of organizations must get comfortable with using these methods to demonstrate their work and their impact. And as funding for the arts gets tighter, I would urge these institutions to think beyond attendance data as their only goal.

Here are some examples from Ashley's work with arts nonprofits, demonstrating solid goals, objectives, and outcomes:

Goal: To ensure that quality arts experiences and events are available to everyone in the community, regardless of ability to pay or socioeconomic status by providing free or discounted tickets to low-income residents and students.

Objectives:
- To offer free or discounted tickets directly to community residents with household income below the federal poverty line.
- To offer free tickets to low-income community residents through our partnerships with other local community organizations.
- To offer free tickets to low-income students through our partnerships with local schools.

Outcomes:
- 50% of the residents directly offered free or discounted tickets will attend a performance.
- 50% of the residents offered free tickets through a partner organization will attend a performance.

- 60% of the students offered free tickets through a partner school will attend a performance.

With these examples in mind, let's get back to talking about logic models.

To see other examples of logic models, you can do some research on the many great nonprofit websites out there with suggested models you can replicate. Some good websites to check for these purposes are your state's council of nonprofits website (not all states have one, but most do), the National Council of Nonprofits, and also some websites of federal agencies such as the National Endowment for the Arts. If you're having trouble locating a good model with any of these resources, look for local, regional, state, and national programs which are visibly successful at what they do and seek to replicate those.

Finding a model based on best practices and/or with a track record of success is often not just a time-saver, but also a darn good idea since grant makers will love to see that you have taken the time to adapt a proven model for your own program. This dramatically increases your odds of that grant maker viewing your program as a slam dunk of an investment.

The same approach can and should be used not just for designing the program, but also for designing its data collection and evaluation methods. Look for best practices and proven models that can be adapted, but also make sure that they are actually evaluating the best indicators of *your* program's effectiveness. This is where you should go back to the questions listed above and double check that your data supports the need for the program, the impact its making, the wise use of your programs resources, and any other critical elements of your program which need to be communicated to grant makers.

Once you have your basic structure in place for program delivery and evaluation, it's time to streamline, streamline, streamline. Look for tasks that can be automated, forms or procedures that can be combined, interactions with program participants that can be bettered, and ways to generally increase efficiency. Examples could include combining 2 client intake forms which contain redundant information or automating data entry using a program like Zapier so that staff can focus their time on higher-level tasks.

Your efforts should add up to less frustration for program participants, less work for staff, and the same or better results for the overall program. And not surprisingly, the programs that make the biggest impact have worked to make their programs efficient. They spend their time on the activities that matter most; not busy work, redundant tasks, and things that cause frustration for their clients, participants, and patrons.

Lastly, plan for how you will manage grants before you ever get one. Take the time when designing a program to think about how you will protect and organize the data you collect, where the files will live (both hard copies and e-files), how you will schedule and remember important dates and tasks, etc. If you prove to a grant maker that you've put thought into these processes they will be more likely to fund you. Plus, you will be 100% sure at the outset that you do, in fact, actually have the capacity to handle these grants.

When you do get that award and put these measures into practice you'll be actively proving that you are a good steward of grant money. And that, friends, is what helps you get funded over and over again.

All of this is well and good when you are designing a brand spanking new program, but what should you do if you find yourself with an established program and it's becoming increasingly clear that it isn't up to snuff in terms of design and evaluation? Approach it as if it's new.

First, establish that the need for the program does still exist and that its current model is well-suited to addressing that need. If it *isn't*, then it's time to use the steps outlined above to find a model that will better deliver results. The same goes for evaluation methods. Yes, this may be time-consuming, frustrating work and you may end up completely revamping a beloved core program (which makes many of us sick to our stomachs).

But ask yourself this: would you rather do that hard work or continue running an ineffectual program until community support and funding dries up because *everyone else* knows it isn't making the grade? Your choice (but it should be an easy one).

In many cases, the outcomes you measure will be pretty straightforward and based on common sense. To give you more examples, Bruce used to write grant proposals for a supportive housing program benefiting homeless individuals and families. The program consisted of transitional housing, where residency could last no longer than 24 months, and permanent supportive housing, where residents could stay as long as they wanted, provided they met the income requirements. He used the following benchmarks for measuring success in relation to this program:

- 60% of residents who leave the transitional housing units will have obtained permanent housing;
- 60% of permanent housing residents will remain housed for at least 6 months;
- 60% will have employment as a source of income at the time of exit; and
- 75% will make regular rent payments.

We are not saying you should use these exact outcomes if you work for a housing program. We are providing this simply for instructional purposes.

Even straightforward outcomes like this can pose challenges. Sometimes, program staff did not know the destination of residents who exited the program, who usually left suddenly. When this housing program was smaller, the outcomes could skew easily in either direction due to the small number of residents involved. Simple explanations will usually suffice in such cases. If you fell considerably short of an outcome, explain what you think caused it and how you plan to address it. It's not fun to have to report a substandard outcome to a foundation, but it does happen, and you need to proactively address it for both grant and program improvement purposes.

Chapter 4:
Diversity on Multiple Fronts

Your organization needs diversity in more ways than one in order to be a viable candidate for foundation grants. You may still get grants if you fall short in one or more of these areas, but you're better off addressing each of these areas as much as possible.

<u>Racial, ethnic, and gender diversity</u>. Bruce once worked with a nonprofit organization in an urban area that had been around for a few decades, but had only recently sought foundation grants in a systematic way. A large local foundation conducted a site visit in response to a grant proposal submitted by the organization.

The site visit went well, except for one aspect. When the foundation officer learned that all nine board members were Caucasian and only one was a woman, she flatly told the organization they needed more women and members of minority groups represented on their board. Fortunately, the organization still received a much-needed grant from this funder. However, the grant amount was considerably less than requested. Clearly, they were sending a message along with the grant check.

Diversity of thought. With reason, your organization needs a healthy exchange of ideas, which can be and often is characterized by a certain degree of conflict. Not the angry, backstabbing kind of drama that's often found in dysfunctional organizations, but the healthier kind of conflict that wards off groupthink and allows your organization to change with the times.

Diversified sources of funding. Subjectively, if grants comprise more than 25% of your organization's revenue, you may be dangerously dependent on grants. Even stable and strong organizations with good grant writers have good years and not-so-good years when it comes to getting grants in the door. The number of grants you receive and the amounts of those grants depend on so many factors, such as how appealing a program or project is to funders.

The numbers vary a bit from one year to the next. But generally, almost half of nonprofits' total revenue comes from fees for services, be it fees charged directly to those receiving services or payments from Medicaid, Medicare, or private insurance. Donations from individuals comprise 71% of charitable contributions to nonprofits. Foundation grants comprise only a small portion of the overall dollars going into nonprofits' coffers. You need a plan for how you are going to support your services from multiple types of funding sources. Then, you have to carry it out.

<u>Diversified ways of communicating with funders and the general public.</u> Grant proposals should never be the only way a foundation can learn about your organization.

You need a website. This may sound like astonishingly obvious advice, but Bruce recently had to tell an organization they needed a website before they could realistically apply for grants. Foundations want to see how you represent your organization to literally the whole world.

Your online representation will be deemed lacking if your website has no newsletters or annual reports, or if the most recent newsletter and annual report posted on your site are three years old. In addition to posting them on your website, newsletters and annual reports should also be sent to your lists by email and mail. True, "snail mail" is costly and less environmentally friendly. Chances are, a lot of your donors are older, and snail mail is how a lot of older donors prefer to receive communication from your organization.

Snail mail is also how a lot of older donors prefer to make donations. So, contrary to popular myth, direct mail fundraising remains alive and well. You ignore this as a source of support at your peril.

The quality of your written material matters, too. You may think we just stated the obvious in the prior sentence, but we see too much pitiful writing that nonprofits inflict upon the world.

For example, Bruce thinks newsletters and annual reports featuring the "Letter from the Executive Director" or the "Thoughts from the Board President" tripe should be outlawed. That screams "boring prose ahead" like nothing else does. People are too wrapped up in their own lives to give a crap how your board president views the 0.214% decrease in revenue.

We may cover this more extensively in a future book. For an overview like this, though, suffice it to say you should do the following in your organization's written materials:

- Ditch the long or wordy copy.
- Use short articles or descriptions.
- Use simple language a 7th grader can understand.
- Get rid of jargon and hopelessly overused words like "utilize."
- Use visually appealing pictures and graphics.
- Focus on what is likely to interest your reader, not on what you think the reader ought to be interested in.
- It's up to you whether to acknowledge donors in your newsletter or annual report. Wherever you choose to do it, do it consistently.

Chapter 5:
A Note to New Nonprofits (and to Those Thinking About Starting One)

Freelance grant writing consultants often get calls from newly formed nonprofits. Some of these new organizations have proof of their 501(c)(3) nonprofit status from the IRS. Others are a formally established organization, but either have not yet applied for 501(c)(3) status or they have applied, but are waiting for the IRS to send written confirmation of their nonprofit status. We also get calls from people thinking about forming their own nonprofit organization, but who have taken no steps in that direction.

If you fit one of these categories, this chapter is for you, and the first thing we want to say to you is this – <u>you are a badass</u>!

It takes guts and a heart of gold to form a nonprofit. It requires much more of the same to keep it going through a lot of lean years before your organization makes the impact you hoped it would.

All nonprofits had to start somewhere. Some began with plenty of financial resources. Usually, though, nonprofits are founded with a lot of hope but few assets.

However...(surely you knew some form of the word "but" was coming, right?)

We are surprised by how many new nonprofits fail to do their homework before calling us. With very occasional exceptions, the newly formed organizations who call us do not have one or more (usually more) of the following:

- A strategic/business plan of any sort;
- A fundraising plan;
- If applicable, a plan for how they will generate revenue outside of grants or other types of fundraising;
- A sustainability plan (i.e., how they will keep a program or service going after grant funds have been spent);
- Objective information or data showing the needs and the gaps they will be filling (spoiler alert: your subjective intuition about the need is not good enough);
- Partnerships with other organizations or, in some cases, even a history of attempting to collaborate with other organizations;
- Little or no understanding of the information presented in this book about grants; and/or

- Little or no understanding of how difficult it is for larger nonprofits to get grants, let alone new nonprofits with weak infrastructures.

Furthermore, we are astounded by how many nonprofit founders never talk to similar existing organizations <u>before</u> setting up their own nonprofit. Why go through the hassle of starting and running a nonprofit if an established organization is already doing the same activity in your area and might hire you to do it for them?

"Well, Nonprofit ABC isn't doing that activity in this part of town," a founder might say.

Are you sure? Is it possible they're planning to implement that activity in your part of town? Is it possible they haven't secured the funds or the expertise to make it happen? Talk to them!

A founder may reply, "Well, Nonprofit ABC does that activity in my part of town, but the need is so great that my neighborhood needs all the help it can get. Is there some law against having more than one nonprofit doing the same thing in the same geographic area?"

It's perfectly legal for multiple nonprofits to do essentially the same activities in the same geographic areas. There are two potential issues, though.

One, foundations love to see nonprofits collaborating with other organizations. Well-planned and well-run collaborations usually make much more of an impact than a bunch of organizations operating in individual silos. Foundations hate seeing services being duplicated unnecessarily.

Two, you may have a hard time getting grants precisely because another organization already does something similar to you in your geographic area. Suppose you operate a summer camp for low-income youth. If a foundation supports a variety of programs for kids, has already supported three youth summer camps this year, and one of them is in your area and targets largely the same demographics as your camp, getting a grant for your program from that foundation may be a stretch.

We could go on and on with examples like this. Our point is this – there is much more to getting a grant than simply applying for one.

You need plans, an infrastructure, additional ways of generating revenue, and so much more before your new nonprofit is a realistic candidate to receive grants. Once in a really great while, foundations seek new organizations or truly innovative projects in which to invest. By "truly innovative," we mean you have solid evidence of your project's effectiveness and uniqueness as opposed to your mere claim of being innovative.

Otherwise, most foundations are cautious investors who seldom deviate from what is tried and true unless you make it easier for them to say "yes." Your odds of getting a yes improve by following our advice in this book.

Your community needs daring and caring people just like your average nonprofit founder. But you need to do your homework and sweat the small, boring stuff…because the small stuff *is* actually big stuff.

Chapter 6:
How to Find Foundations Who May Support Your Mission

You have all of the documents and verbiage you need to meet the Cain-Ripley definition of "grant ready." You have decided what your desired outcomes are. You have decided how you will measure your outcomes. You are finally ready to find grants, but…where do you find the foundations who might give them to your organization?

You should use some combination of all the following means, below:

Subscription search engines: Bruce used FoundationSearch (www.foundationsearch.com) at a previous job. This is a subscription search engine available through a Canadian company, Metasoft. Their staff will be glad to take you on a thorough, guided tour of FoundationSearch. Another popular subscription search engine is Foundation Directory Online (https://foundationcenter.org/products/foundation-directory-online), available through the Foundation Center (https://foundationcenter.org/), a clearinghouse of information on philanthropy and fundraising. GrantStation is another solid choice. There may be other similar search engines, but these are the ones with which we are familiar.

Basically, FoundationSearch and Foundation Directory Online pull data from foundations' IRS Form 990s. This allows you to find information about the grants they have awarded in a tiny fraction of the time it would take you to sift through each Form 990 on your own. You can conduct your research from a variety of angles. You can search for a particular foundation, you can search for foundations who support a given type of program or organization (arts, human services, religion, etc.) in a broad or limited geographic area, or you can enter the name of an organization similar to yours and see where their grants are coming from.

These search engines are fun to use, but subscriptions are expensive. Fortunately, some libraries offer free access to Foundation Directory Online. See if a library close to you offers free access.

Foundations' websites and social media accounts (if they have them). Most foundations do not have websites or a social media presence. Foundations who give only to pre-selected organizations have no need for a website. Others are smaller family foundations who do not have the time or inclination to maintain a website.

However, a number of foundations do have websites with information about their guidelines, deadlines, and preferences, so it is certainly worth your while to look for them. Some foundations also maintain a social media presence, so that is another way to stay abreast in real time about their giving.

<u>Other nonprofits' websites and social media</u>: Subscription search engines offer tremendous advantages. However, you may occasionally miss prospects such as corporations who do not maintain an associated foundation. When Bruce used FoundationSearch in the past, grants less than $4,000 did not show up in search results.

Hence, searching other nonprofits' websites for grant prospects is a valuable use of your time. Most nonprofits post annual reports, newsletters, or news releases listing who has contributed financially to the organization. Pay special attention to organizations providing the same service(s) as your nonprofit and to organizations in your geographic area operating in the same broad area (arts, human services, health, etc.) as your organization.

While you're perusing other organizations' websites, take note of what material appealed to you versus what was boring. Study the captivating material and adapt accordingly.

<u>Guidestar</u> (www.guidestar.org). Guidestar is an online clearinghouse of nonprofit data. Just set up a free account, and you can access three years' worth of any

nonprofit's IRS Form 990s for free. Guidestar also sells materials, but for just the most recent Form 990s, a free account is all you need.

You can search for a specific foundation. Or, you can search more generally. For example, you can enter the word "foundation" in the search tab, then choose a state, or a city and state to narrow down your search by geography. Bear in mind, though, that some organizations with the word "foundation" in their name are not grant-giving organizations. You can also try using terms such as "trust" or "charitable trust."

One you're looking at a foundation's IRS Form 990, go to page 10 and look at Part XV where it says, "Check here if the foundation only makes contributions to pre-selected charitable organizations and does not accept unsolicited requests for funds." If this box is checked, they do not accept unsolicited grant requests. Later in the Form 990, you will normally find a list of grants given by the foundation, the recipient, the amounts awarded, and possibly a very short description of what program or service the grant supported.

<u>Relevant newsletters.</u> Here in the Cincinnati area, one foundation issues an e-zine that sometimes mentions funding opportunities (both theirs and other foundations). Another free e-zine about the local philanthropy scene contains announcements submitted by nonprofits about grants they have received. Chances

are, your area or state has similar e-zines or paper magazines.

<u>The old-fashioned way</u>, word of mouth. We get tips about possible funders from people at the organizations with whom we work, fundraisers, other grant writers, and even friends and neighbors!

Most tips we get do not break any new ground. Usually, we are already aware of the funder mentioned to us. In other cases, the recommendations are along the lines of, "You should see if _____ (insert name of celebrity here) has a foundation since he lives near you!" Listen patiently anyway. The occasional time you do get a really good tip makes it worth your while to do so.

Chapter 7:
The Nuts and Bolts of Grant Writing

How to Submit Your Applications

Normally, you will submit your foundation grant proposals via one of three ways:

<u>Online portals:</u> Many foundations, particularly larger ones, require applicants to submit grant requests via online portals. Foundations with online portals rarely give you a choice about submitting your grant application any other way. Frequently, you will need to set up an account with a username and password.

You can copy and paste your narrative from a Word document into the portal. Just make sure you're copying and pasting into the correct section of your online application! Typically, you will upload documents such as your board roster, financials, and proof of your nonprofit status into specified sections of the portal. Pay attention to whether the funder requires you to use a form they provide for your financials.

In addition to saving you the hassle and expense of printing out reams of paper and mailing it to them, online application systems prevent grant writers from developing verbal diarrhea. Funders love this feature for that reason. Most systems allow you to enter only so many characters in response to each question. Depending on how much information a given question is trying to elicit, you may be restricted to anything from 250 characters to 4,000 characters, and even more for longer applications. Occasionally, online systems impose words limits as opposed to character limits. Otherwise, character limits are the norm. You will invariably encounter some with pretty severe character limits at that.

In the end, though, character limits are a blessing in disguise for grant writers. They force us to be concise and to keep it simple, a good strategy no matter what format you must use.

Email: Some foundations require you, or give you the option of emailing your grant applications to them.

Snail mail: A number of foundations, particularly smaller ones, still require applicants to apply by mail. Express mail is usually not necessary, unless time leaves you no choice. Express mail is expensive to boot. You're better off using priority mail.

Whether the funder requires you to submit your grant proposal via an online system, email, or snail mail, pay close attention to the funder's instructions. One Cincinnati area foundation specifically prohibits you from using express mail to send your proposals. We assume this is because there may or may not be anyone at their office to sign for it. Another local foundation asks you to make sure your emailed proposals are scanned in black and white. Why risk irritating the funder because you did not pay attention to small details which, in the grant world, can really be big details? In this arena, attention to detail will often make the difference in who gets the grant and who gets denied.

Below, some of the questions or components may not be required by a particular funder. Or, the funder imposes such severe space limitations that you cannot possibly include everything you desire. However, we are presenting some questions you might see from a funder who requires a lot of information.

Letter of Intent

A letter of intent (also sometimes referred to as an "LOI" for short) is sometimes the initial step in the process of applying for a grant. Usually, but not always, a letter of intent is a 1-2 page letter that briefly describes your organization, your project or program, and how you would spend a grant if you were invited to submit a full proposal that results in a grant.

Some funders offer specific instructions about what they want to see in your letter of intent, how long they want the letter to be and what, if anything, you should attach to the letter. Some letters of intent are completed in funders' online application system, where the parameters are set for you. With online submissions, letters of intent often look more like a short grant application.

With a letter of intent, you have one goal, and one goal only – to be invited to submit a full grant proposal to that funder. You have to make every word count, since letters of intent are almost always short.

Part of passing this hurdle involves just following simple instructions. If the funder asks for a one-page letter, give it to them. Do *not* give them a three page letter with attachments. If they ask for you to provide your mission, IRS determination letter, a short description of your program, and a program budget, then provide just that. You are in the beginning stages of creating this relationship. Don't annoy them by overloading them with information they don't want.

And, for goodness sakes, make sure a letter of intent submitted by mail is addressed to an actual human who is currently affiliated with that foundation. Do not address it to 'Whom it May Concern'! Possibly, your research did not reveal any information on what to send them and you haven't been successful in contacting them by phone or even by email. When that is the case, Ashley has had success in sending a cover letter and a short proposal (no more than a few pages) with the mission, a description of the program, objectives and outcomes, a short program budget, and a short description of how grant funds would be used. Make sure you include your contact information and let them know in your letter that you will be following up.

Cover letter

You probably will not be able to include a cover letter with a proposal submitted through an online application system. Otherwise, assume a snail-mailed or emailed proposal needs a cover letter unless something in the funder's instructions indicates this is a bad idea (for example, if they say "Send **only** the following documents…" and a cover letter is not a document they listed).

When including a cover letter is permissible, here are guidelines to which you should adhere:

- Limit your cover letter to one page.
- Put it on your organization's letterhead.
- Only a person with authority to sign documents on your organization's behalf (usually the executive director and/or board president) should sign it.
- Do not have more than one person sign it, unless a funder requires two signatures (for example, from both your executive director and board president).

- Mention your organization's name, the grant amount being requested and, in a few words or 1-2 sentences, how you will use the grant.
- If applicable, make reference to the Foundation's past support of your organization. Foundation staff members or board members reading your cover letter may not always immediately recall they supported your organization in the past. Making a brief reference to past support signals that if your organization was worthy of support in the past, then perhaps that is the case now as well.

Otherwise, the format is largely up to you. Here is an example of a cover letter Bruce used in the past, with some details changed:

Dear Ms. Smith:

When most people think of the homeless, they envision an older man living on the streets. But in Northern Kentucky, you're probably as likely to see a woman who is homeless.

They could be in any number of situations – fleeing domestic violence...sleeping in abandoned cars...or on the verge of eviction with nowhere to go. The bottom line is they're homeless with no apparent end in sight.

A collaborative effort called Project ABC is doing something about this problem in Covington. Through this project, Awesome Organization and two partner agencies have provided that "end in sight" for countless homeless women and children since 1994.

Awesome Organization is requesting a $5,000 grant from The Generous Foundation to support the substance abuse treatment and childcare we provide to project participants at our Experience Strength & Hope Program in Covington. The Foundation has generously supported Awesome Organization's mission in the past, and we hope you can help once again.

Thank you for considering an investment in the well-being of the homeless women and children we serve. Please contact Bruce Ripley at (XXX)XXX-XXXX or at bripley@awesomeorganization.org if you have questions.

Sincerely,

Dudley DoRight
Executive Director
Awesome Organization

Executive Summary

An executive summary is sometimes, but not typically required by foundations.

If the funder does not say what they want in your executive summary, think of it as the 1-page version of your overall grant proposal. Consider the example below, based on an actual executive summary written by Bruce when the opioid epidemic had just become front page news:

The focus of this request is Awesome Organization's Detoxification Unit ("Detox Unit") in Any City, USA. This program accommodates up to 8 men and 4 women at a time who need support during withdrawal from alcohol and other drugs. The unit admits clients 24 hours per day for periods of 7-14 days.

Most of those admitted to the unit are low-income. Most are homeless. The program serves around 500 people a year. While in our unit, clients receive a physical exam and attend classes and self-help recovery groups.

Just as many hospital patients are first seen in the emergency room, many of our residential and outpatient substance abuse treatment clients were first seen in our Detox Unit. The program is a vital first step toward recovery.

Last year, 98% of those admitted safely underwent withdrawal without needing hospital care. The Detox Unit is considerably less expensive than hospital detoxification, so our unit saves taxpayers almost $1 million a year because it reduces the burden on the state's indigent care fund.

The Detox Unit is on the front lines of the heroin epidemic underway in Any City, USA. More than 80% of those admitted to the program are addicted to heroin. Several factors are fueling the rise of heroin addiction. Prescription painkillers such as OxyContin have become more difficult to obtain, heroin is more potent than ever, and intense cravings make it hard to quit. It has become something of a "mainstream" drug, as the epidemic impacts low-income, middle class, and high-income households alike.

This is the context in which we are requesting a $10,000 grant. If awarded a grant, Awesome Organization will use it to support the existing services at the Detox Unit, where expenses always exceeded revenue.

Awesome Organization is uniquely qualified to offer this program. With a $7.1 million budget and 135 staff members, we provide annually more than 140,000 days of care in our residential programs, in addition to providing outpatient counseling. This is more residential services than any other organization, including hospitals, in Any City, USA and at a fraction of the cost at hospitals or for-profit facilities.

In cases where you include an executive summary, this could be the only part of the proposal some of the reviewers read. Make it count.

Mission Statement and Organization Overview

Every grant proposal should contain your mission statement. So, make sure your mission statement isn't boring or clunky. What you write in the organizational overview will depend partly on how much space you have, but generally, the overview of your organization should contain information such as the following:

- The year the organization was founded
- A bit about your organization's history. Mention any humble origins associated with your organization, such as beginning operations in a church basement. Mention what need your organization was founded to meet.
- Current organizational budget
- Number of staff and/or volunteers
- Brief descriptions of programs or types of services offered by your organization.

If space allows, you can also mention social proof type items such as recent honors received by your organization or recent inspection results from a licensing or accreditation body. It always helps if you can say a third party vouched for how awesome your organization is.

Ideally, this section will be around ½ to ¾ of a page long. Of course, if the funder wants more than this, give it to them. Give a good idea of who you are and what you do without excessive detail.

Statement of Need/Problem

Here, you will provide evidence of why your services are needed in the geographic area of relevance to your program or project. If you serve one county, provide data showing the need in that county. If you program focuses on one specific census tract, demonstrate the need in that census tract. Unless you are serving the whole nation or an entire state, you should generally stay away from presenting U.S. or state-level data. In the rare instance where reliable local data cannot be found, you can present national or state-level data and make an estimate based on the higher level data. However, you need to say this is how you arrived at the figures you are presenting. Otherwise, make every effort to show the need on the appropriate geographic level.

In addition to using data from needs assessments or publicly available data, your organization's internal data can help make your case. How many people do you have on your waiting list? How many participants are presenting with the issue that a new program would solve? Look at what, if any numbers you already have.

Ideally and if applicable, mention what you have already done to address the problem. For example, "To address homelessness in Cincinnati, Awesome Organization has created 28 units of supportive housing in the last 3 years. However, the need for supportive housing still outstrips the supply. Last year's point-in-time survey counted 547 people living on the streets or in shelters. Since point-in-time surveys only count people who could be located on that day, the actual number is believed to be significantly higher. This is the context in which we are requesting a $50,000 grant."

Project/Program Description

Write the description of the program/project for which you are seeking funds so a person of average intelligence who is unfamiliar with it understands what you want to do. This advice applies to your grant proposals as a whole. However, it especially applies here because the program/project you're describing is what you are asking the funder to support. Do not leave the funder confused about what you want to do.

Some grant application forms may ask more specific questions within the program/project description section. Assuming space permits, you should try provide this information to the extent possible:

Summary of program/project. Keep it simple. Answer basic questions nearly anyone would have, such as where the program/project will take place, how many people will benefit and, if applicable, demographic data (age range, race/ethnicity breakdown, etc.) on who will benefit. Include your best estimate of how many people will benefit from the program or project at a given time, over the course of a year, or over the course of multiple years if you can say. Some people reviewing your proposal may judge it partly on how many people will potentially benefit.

However, do not despair if your program serves a small number of people. If this applies to you, explain why this might be the case (for example, your program serves clients with severe and multiple disabilities, which results in you having to spend a lot of money in order to serve a single client).

<u>The proposed use of grant funds</u>. If grant funds will support an existing program in its current form, say so. You can strengthen your response by saying something like, "If awarded a $20,000 grant, $17,500 will be used toward personnel costs and $2,500 will be used toward program supplies not covered by other funding sources." Say something like this only if it is true, though. If you're seeking grants for a renovation project, say so. If you know exactly how much various supplies and materials will cost, you can spell it out. However, if a contractor is doing the work and you cannot realistically give a breakdown of labor, materials, and so on, just say the grant will support renovation costs.

<u>Timetable for implementation</u>. Obviously, this does not apply if the grant will support an existing program. If the grant will support a program or program expansion that does not exist yet, give a realistic estimate of when

you will open or expand the program. Here, we emphasize the word "realistic." Allow time for something to go wrong when opening a program or completing a capital project...because something usually does go wrong. Provide your best, good-faith estimate here.

Duration of program/project. If it's a time limited project or program, such as a renovation project or an orchestra's music season, let them know the projected time frame.

Evidence of use of best practices.
What are the odds your program is likely to be effective with the audience you intend to serve? How do you know this? There *is* evidence supporting the effectiveness of your program and/or specific activities/practices within your program, correct?

This is where the use of best practices and evidence-based practices comes in.

The concept of evidence-based practices is reported to have originated in medicine in the early 1990s, where it was called evidence based medicine. The concept later spread to other fields such as education and addiction treatment. Evidence based practices are normally determined in relation to what is the best available research evidence about whether or why a program, treatment, service or intervention works, and whether or why it works with certain populations.

In an ideal world, you researched this before you decided to start this program and the program design is based off what you found in your research. If you didn't, then Google is your friend. Find a reputable authority in your field who has identified your program or specific activities as a best practice. Find academic research supporting the utility of what you plan to do. If academic research is not plentiful or does not exist, see what a relevant professional association or institute has identified as services or program models that should be replicated. If you are replicating a program that has been successfully implemented elsewhere, tell the funder this and explain why you believe the program will succeed in your location.

For nonprofits in the arts & culture arena, you can find a wealth of data, research, and information on best practices and evidence-based models on the websites of the National Endowment for the Arts, the National Endowment for the Humanities, and many state Arts Councils. You can also often find information on best practices that apply to nonprofits of every stripe on the National Council of Nonprofits website (as well as on many of the state Council of Nonprofit websites).

If what you are proposing is evidence-based but you are deviating from aspects of a proven program, explain why. The good news is you may be able to get a grant to support the planning phase (for example, by hiring a contract facilitator to lead your organization through the planning process).

Foundations get far more grant requests than they could ever hope to fund. Your job is to show them your program is a good investment.

Collaboration with other organizations. Funders like to see collaboration. It shows you're working with the larger community to benefit your constituents while (at least in theory) pooling resources and reducing unnecessary duplications of services. List only those organizations with whom you are truly collaborating. Mention instances where you have a signed memorandum of agreement (MOA), a memorandum of understanding (MOU), or some type of formal agreement with other organizations to serve people who may need services from your organization plus the other organization. This shows you have more than just a loose, informal collaboration.

If you aren't sure how to write an MOA or MOU, never fear. There are a million good resources on the internet to get you started (just Google "Nonprofit Memorandum of Understanding"). Many funders also have templates you can use or you could ask a nonprofit colleague if you can see an example that you could repurpose.

By the way, this seems like a good place to give the following advice…never collaborate with another organization solely for the purpose of getting a grant. Only collaborate when it truly makes sense to do so. Funders can spot CINOs (Collaborations in Name Only) from a mile away. You'll irritate them and possibly not get a grant.

Agency's qualifications and appropriateness to address the need. When space permits, write at least a few sentences describing how your organization is uniquely qualified to provide the program/service in question. If your organization has stability at the executive level, this can be a good place to mention how long your chief executive officer, chief operating officer, and/or chief financial officer have been with the organization or in their respective positions at your organization.

Evaluation

Depending on space and the foundation's requirements, provide the grant maker with at least your top three intended outcomes. If you're writing for a health or human services program, your outcomes should provide an indication of how participants will be changed by the program/project. Examples include:

- "80% of participants will score higher on a post-test than on a pre-test measuring ABC."
- "Increase the percentage of clients with employment as a source of income from 50% to 80% by the end of the 1-year reporting period."

- "85% of children are assessed age-appropriate in social and emotional development or meet at least 67% of Individual Family Service Plan (IFSP) or Individualized Educational Plan (IEP) goals"

If you are writing for an arts, culture, or humanities program, your outcomes should still reflect how patrons or the community would be changed as a result of the program. (In other words, don't write outcomes which only talk about how many butts you got to fill the seats or vague outcomes that could never be measured). Here are some examples:
- 80% of students attending events through partnerships with their school will have a deepened understanding of various performance mediums as well as individual works, as evidenced by pre- and post-test surveys given at the beginning and end of the performance season.
- 90% of students participating in the arts administration job shadowing program will have a better understanding of careers and opportunities available to them as well as a better understanding of how to perform required job tasks for those careers.
- There will be a 5% decrease in neighborhood unemployment rates, attributable directly to increased tourism and spending generated by the

arts organizations in the neighborhood, including XYZ Org.

If writing about a capital project, you can present your outcomes in one of two ways:

1) Simply say, "Our primary goal is to finish XYZ Project on time and within the projected budget." That is your goal, correct?

2) Or, you can say, "Our primary goal is to finish XYZ Project on time and within the projected budget," then go on to say what your intended outcomes are for the program related to the capital request. Unless space prohibits us from doing so, we are partial to this option. The more you can do to generate the funder's interest in your program-to-be, the better.

When space permits, tell the funder how the evaluation will be conducted. Normally, all you need here is a short description. Here are a couple examples:

- Housing program staff regularly compile information related to these outcomes and enter the data into the state's database for social services and housing providers who serve the homeless.

- Professional assessment results, such as the occupational therapist's assessment, and progress toward goals outlined in each child's

Individual Family Service Plans and Individualized Educational Plans are used to measure success.

- Community arts center staff routinely compile and analyze satisfaction surveys given to arts class students in order to continually improve class offerings.

- Survey feedback and grade reports from school counselors are used to determine the effectiveness of arts programming as a factor in increasing grades and graduation rates.

Foundations like to see evidence your clients/patrons/constituents are involved in your program evaluation and in your organization in general. Do your clients participate in exit interviews before leaving your program? Do you conduct focus groups with your target audience? Are past recipients of services on your board of directors or employed in the program? Do you have a client advisory board?

Mention at least briefly how you will use your evaluation results and how you will disseminate them. Ideally, you are disseminating your results via reports to funders, annual reports, newsletters, and/or social media. Ideally, you are also using evaluation results as a tool for making necessary changes to your programming.

Finally, if space and guidelines permit, mention your most recent set of outcomes if you are seeking funds to support an existing program.

Other Prospective or Actual Funders of Your Program/Project

Grant makers like to see that you have sought or will seek grants from other funders. Typically, foundations do not like to be the sole source of support for a program or project. You should list the name of the foundation, how much you requested/will request, and what the status of that request is (awarded $10,000, declined, pending). Below is an example of Bruce's from several years ago.

Source	**Amount Requested/to be Requested**	Status
Butler Foundation	$7,500	Pending
Fifth Third Foundation	$10,000	To be submitted by 4/10
Grant Foundation	$10,000	To be submitted by 5/10

Greater Cincinnati Foundation	$5,000	Awarded a $20,000 "Weathering the Economic Storm" grant in 12/09. Of this, $5,000 was earmarked for Program ABC
Hatton Foundation	$10,000	To be submitted by 4/10
Scripps Howard Foundation	$5,000	To be submitted by 4/10
Spaulding Foundation	$20,000	To be submitted by 6/10
Wohlgemuth Herschede Fdn.	10,000	To be submitted by 4/10

Other Anticipated Funding:

To the extent possible, funders also like to see you are using non-grant funding sources to support your program or project. List potential sources for your program or project such as earned revenue, in-kind support, special events, donations, and fundraisers such as your annual fund drive, along with amounts from each category. Make sure the dollar amounts you list here match what you say in your program/project budget.

How you will sustain the program or project:

If you are requesting funds for a temporary project, such as a pilot program or a capital project, simply say this is not applicable. However, if the capital project is supporting an eventual program, an expansion of a program, or even just your organization in general, you should go on to say how you are going to sustain the program or your organization's overall services in the long run. Describe, wherever applicable, whether earned revenue, donations, special events, or other non-grant sources of funding will be used to sustain the program.

If you plan to continue applying for grants, mention that as well. However, your program/project may not appeal to funders if you are going to rely heavily or exclusively on foundation grants to keep it going. The number of foundation grants and the overall amount you raise from grant writing can vary widely from one year to the next. You really need more funding sources than just grants to keep a program going.

You can also indicate how you will sustain your organization in non-financial ways. For example, the organization where Bruce works part-time offers an intensive in-house leadership training program for staff members who meet certain criteria and are interested in management positions within the organization. Obviously, strengthening your pool of potential future managers is good for an organization's sustainability.

Unfortunately, some grant writers use this section to try out their fiction writing skills when they, or the organization, has a vague or no idea how they will sustain a program after the grant funds have been expended.

Do not take this route. Foundation officers and board members are savvy investors. One reason why they are (usually) wealthy is they can smell BS from a mile away. Remember, we told you previously that a plan for how you will sustain services after a grant ends is essential for new nonprofits. It is equally essential for established nonprofit organizations, too. If you realistically evaluate your options, yet remain flummoxed about how you are going to sustain your program, take a hard look at whether you should implement this program in the first place.

Chapter 8:
General Writing Tips

We've said it before and we'll say it again - keep it simple. When you write a grant proposal, you are not writing for a literary prize. You're writing for results. Here are ways you can keep it simple:

Use simple, direct language. For example, instead of saying "We will utilize…," say "We will use…"

See through the funder's eyes. Almost without exception, foundations get far more grant requests than they could ever hope to fund. This means they have to read a lot of grant proposals. When you prepare a grant proposal, you will get a lot of information thrown at you by your program staff and others. Once you get that information, it is your job to shape the narrative such that an outside person of at least average intelligence can read it and understand your organization and what you want to do with a grant.

Obviously, you have to think about your program and your organization when you write grant proposals, but you also need to think about the people reading your grant proposals. Foundation staff and board members enjoy the feeling of doing good, just like you. By telling them about the great work your organization does or wants to do, you are affording them an opportunity to feel good. Talk about what is important to them. This is easier to do when the foundation has publicly stated what their funding preferences are, but you can do this to some extent just by looking at their giving history. If the foundation funds children's programs, and your organization serves both children and adults, tell them how their grant will benefit children. When possible and appropriate, give them a real example of a child you've helped and include a picture or two.

<u>Edit ruthlessly,</u> whether or not online application character limits force you to do so. One sort of easy way to tighten up your writing is to cut 95% of the adjectives and adverbs from your first draft. We say "sort of" because for whatever reason, grant writers (including us) get kind of emotionally attached to the way we have phrased certain sentences, paragraphs, or sections.

However, like we said before, you are not writing for literary acclaim. You are writing for results. The best way to get the result you want is to make as few mistakes as possible. Proposals should be typo-free, grammatically correct, and generally easy for the other person to understand. Loosening any emotional attachment you have to your prose will only help.

Trust us – the republic will remain standing if you write about "Program ABC" instead of "the exceptionally unique Program ABC."

<u>Be environmentally unfriendly.</u> We almost hate to disclose this, but Bruce frequently prints out his proposals during the editing process. When you are constantly looking at a computer screen, issues with what you have written have a way of hiding in plain sight, probably due to becoming desensitized. When you print out your draft and literally look at it from a different angle, you may catch things you had been missing over and over.

<u>Say it loud, say it proud!</u> Bruce once landed a gig as a keynote speaker at a conference. He didn't realize how bad the first draft of his speech was until he read it out loud. Sentences that seemed like slick prose on paper made Bruce sound like a windbag when he spoke them. Chances are, you'll feel like a dork when you read it out loud, but it does help. Try it.

Chapter 9:
Cultivating Relationships with Grant Makers

Relationships are everything in the nonprofit world. Relationships with your community, with those you serve, with local officials, with other organizations, and with your donors are all crucial to your nonprofit's success. Relationships with grant makers are no different.

Your nonprofit most likely has a process they use to identify donors, establish a relationship with them, solicit a donation, and then continue evolving the relationship so that the donor continues to give and/or increases their giving over the years. You should develop a similar process for cultivating relationships with grant makers.

That process should look something like this:

Here are all the details for how to work this process and create beneficial relationships with grant makers:

Research

This is the stage where the grant maker likely doesn't know much, if anything, about your organization and you should also be learning as much as you can about them, too. Start by doing your homework. You should research the history of their foundation, its funding interests, eligibility criteria, as well as its board members. And of course, you should look at 990s. We recommend looking at several years' worth of 990s to get a clear picture of the foundation's giving history. Do a quick Google search for them as well. Sometimes you find great information that way!

Part of your research phase should also be identifying the best way to make contact. This can be done in two ways: through the foundation's paid staff or through its board members. If a foundation *has* paid staff, you should always attempt to contact them first. This ensures that staff aren't given the impression that you are doing an end run around them to reach the board and influence funding decisions. It will also ensure that you don't annoy board members who expect inquiries to go through the staff.

However, many foundations are small and do not have any staff on board to field inquiries. When this is the case, take a close look at who sits on their board as well as any affiliations they may hold (employers, professional organizations, memberships, etc.). Do any of your staff or board members know anyone on their board? If so, ask them to make an introduction. If not, look for other opportunities to get to know them. This could be done by attending a meeting or presentation they are also attending or even applying to be a speaker at such a meeting. Of course, if you meet someone for the first time in a context like this, do not solicit them or talk grants at that time. Just make the contact and try to set a later date or time to follow up about the grant opportunity.

Next, you should find out if the foundation in question specifies a way they prefer to be approached. Many of them will ask for a letter or a short proposal with very specific information in it as a first approach. You can typically locate this information on their Foundation Directory Online or GrantStation profile or on their website (*if* they have a website).

Initial Contact

Whether you are able to locate information on how to approach them or not, we still think that making an initial contact is vital to creating the type of relationship you want with grant makers. If you've managed to identify a staff or board member with whom your organization has a connection, reach out to them. If not, try to identify a program or grants officer or at least a primary phone number for the organization that you can call.

Make sure you've done your research *before* you ever pick up the phone, though. Many grant makers keep records of contacts from potential grantees and if you appear uninformed about what the foundation cares about or ask a question whose answer is easily found elsewhere, it will make you look unprofessional.

When you call, introduce yourself and make sure this is a good time to talk. If it is, give them a brief overview of what your organization does. Let them know that you have done some research about their foundation and believe that their interests and your program could be a great match. Ask if they would be interested in hearing more about your programs and receiving a proposal.

At this point, the conversation could go either way. If they believe it isn't a good match, thank them for the time and move on. If they *are* interested, you should take this time to confirm some details with them. If your research didn't reveal any information on how to apply, ask them if they have a specific application process or format you should use. If you *did* find this information, confirm that it's still correct. Also confirm that you have correct submission deadlines. If they have no specific deadlines, ask what time might be best for them to receive your proposal.

Taking the time to have this conversation does 2 things: it shows that you are diligent and thorough in your approach to grant writing (which bodes well if you become a grantee) and it helps you stand out from the crowd of other applicants (because believe us when we say they are *not* all making this call).

Proposal/Letter of Intent (LOI)

When you are able to locate information detailing how to approach a foundation and/or you've been given this information after your initial contact, your job is to follow it to the letter. Like we said before, give them the information or material they requested, and nothing more! Throwing everything but the kitchen sink at them will not make your case.

The one area where you have wiggle room is the cover letter. Even if a cover letter was not a required part of the application, send one that is brief and engaging. It's good manners and is another way for you to stand out from the pack.

As stated earlier, it's also possible your research did not reveal any information on what to send them and you haven't been successful in contacting them by phone or even by email. In which case, just send a cover letter and a short proposal (no more than a few pages) with the mission, a description of the program, objectives and outcomes, a short program budget, and a short description of how grant funds would be used. Make sure you include your contact information and let them know in your letter that you will be following up.

Follow-Ups
Plan to call your foundation contact again a week or two after you submit your letter or proposal. At this time, ask if they have any questions or if there are any additional materials they would like. You can also ask if they know when a decision will be made, if that information wasn't outlined elsewhere.

It's possible, even likely, that it's too soon for anyone to have thoroughly reviewed your proposal at this point. However, this call is still important as it further establishes in their minds that you are a committed and accessible partner should they fund your program.

Next up will be the moment of truth. Did you get that grant award or not?

<u>When you don't get the grant...</u>
Don't throw things, don't have a temper tantrum, and certainly don't write off that grant maker as a lost cause. Rather, call or email them again. Not all of them will take the time to reply or return messages, but it's still worth the effort. It shows that you cared about the

grant and the relationship with the funder and it shows a willingness to improve. When you reach out to them, ask the following questions:

1. What could you have done differently with your proposal, LOI, or your approach?
2. What did they like about your proposal? What did they dislike?
3. Would a different program have been more competitive?
4. Would another proposal be welcome during their next round?
5. Do they have any other feedback that would help?
6. Can they recommend any other grant makers that might be interested in your program or organization?

All declined proposals are an opportunity. Although your instinct may be to throw the file in the trash and never think of that funder again, it would be a mistake. Ask them the questions outlined above and use their answers to improve your understanding of writing grants and cultivating relationships. If you do this, then you have still achieved something worthwhile.

<u>When you get the grant...</u>
Receiving a grant award is a cause for great celebration. It also marks the beginning of the hard work, not the

end of it. Of course, you probably already know that now you will need to make good on all of your proposal's promises by running your program, collecting data, and submitting any required reports.

However, you will also need to have a plan for thanking your funder(s) and nurturing this new relationship. And you will likely need to have several strategies for doing so, not just one.

Your first stop in formulating your "Thank You Strategy" should be the grant agreement. Often it will outline some of the ways in which you are required to recognize or thank your donor. This could include signage at a particular event or inclusion of their logo in relevant marketing materials. The wording of the grant agreement should spell out these requirements and if anything is unclear or not addressed, you should definitely call your contact person at the foundation and ask.

In addition to any required acknowledgements, there are additional thank you methods you can and should add to your to-do list. Below, they are broken out into "must-do's" and "nice touches".

Thank You Must-Do's:
- Initial thank you call
- Thank you letter.

- Update calls, emails or letters, depending on how the funder prefers to be contacted.
- Make sure the foundation is ok with publicity about their grant. Some foundations want to remain anonymous and do not allow you to publicly acknowledge them at all. Others want to see a draft of your press release before you issue it. A few foundations require you to use very exact wording in your public statements.

<u>Nice Touches (assuming the funder has no restrictions around publicity):</u>
- Add their logo to your website
- Add their logo to relevant signs
- Write a thank-you blog post
- Write a press release
- Write a series of social media posts, to be spread out over the grant/program period
- Invitation for a site visit and tour
- Send holiday cards
- Send copies of your newsletter
- Send any photos, press clippings, or other materials that demonstrate the impact their funding made
- Verbal thank you's or announcements at relevant moments or events
- Inclusion in annual report, brochures, newsletters, and marketing materials

- Free tickets or invitations to events hosted by your organization

Outline a plan that includes a mix of the suggestions above and then make sure to enter these items into your calendar. After all, if it doesn't get scheduled, it doesn't get done. By taking the time to thank your grant makers, acknowledge their gift, and help give them the "warm and fuzzies" about the impact they are helping you make, you ensure that they think of your organization often and fondly. This is how pros create and sustain relationships with grant makers which pay dividends for years to come.

Chapter 10:
The Ethics of Grant Writing

Ethics is a subject that makes some squeamish, others bored, and still others a little confused as to why we're talking about it in the context of grants. Yet, it's an incredibly important topic for grant writers and nonprofits. After all, you're dealing with the stewardship of money that's been given to you in good faith.

Having said that, grant writing has its own guiding set of principles and ethics. Those who intend to engage in grant writing either as consultants or nonprofit staff would do well to be aware of some do's and don'ts which can help keep them out of some pretty hot water!

The following are our top 5 guidelines for ethical grant writing:

1. **<u>Make sure the information you present is accurate</u>**
   This first guideline should govern everything you write in a grant, from the proposed activities and mission all the way down to nitty gritty details like evaluation plans, budgets, and even bios for key staff. If you present your

program, your organization, or its finances in a less than truthful light, it could lead to your grant funding being revoked once the grant maker learns the truth (and they will).

If you *do* get caught fudging the truth about your program or organization, you will also likely ruin your chances of ever getting another grant from that funder. Often, foundation staff and trustees know the staff and trustees at foundations. As a result, word travels quickly in the foundation community. Your misstep could cost you grant awards with a whole list of funders who now question the veracity of every proposal you submit.

In other words: don't lie and don't stretch the truth. It's not worth it. Make absolutely sure that the information you include in your proposals is truthful, accurate, and true to the spirit of your organization and its work.

2. **Obey the Law (and other rules & regulations)**
    We can practically hear you groaning right now. Telling you to obey the law is a no-brainer. But you'd be surprised how many nonprofits unwittingly get themselves into trouble regardless of how obvious this seems.

    You should always make sure you are aware of any applicable state and federal laws that could affect how you implement a program, manage finances, or collect data. This is especially true in the case of state or federal grants, but absolutely still applies for foundation funding. For example, if your organization intends to partner with local nursing homes to deliver arts classes to Alzheimer's patients, you better make sure that your data collection tools don't violate HIPPA (the Health Insurance Portability & Accountability Act which governs patient privacy).

However, state and federal laws are not the only things on which you should educate yourself. Regulations and rules set out by the grant maker, other organizations you partner with, or local municipalities could also apply. As with many things in life, make sure you do your due diligence by reading *all* the grant application instructions, educating yourself about any local regulations that might come into play, and asking thoughtful questions of partners, lawmakers, and other relevant officials.

If you *are* fortunate enough to receive a grant award, you will often be required to sign a grant agreement. But this is no time to sign your name in a fit of joy without reading the fine print. Make sure you go through the grant agreement and confirm you can uphold its requirements before you sign on the dotted line and send it back to the grant maker.

3. Do what you said you would do

If you write a grant and receive an award it is absolutely vital that you do exactly what you said you would do in your proposal. If you said you intend to give out 500 free tickets to a performance, then you need to do that. If you said you want to evaluate the effectiveness of an after-school mentoring program by tracking the students' grades and other outcome markers, then you better actually track those things!

If you say one thing and do another, odds are the grant maker will find out and you risk losing those grant funds or being required to pay them back. It can destroy your personal reputation as a professional and the reputation of your organization as one worthy of receiving grant funding.

At this point you may be thinking "ok, but sometimes things don't go as planned." You're right. Any number of things can throw a monkey wrench into your plans. If this happens to you, you should communicate as early as possible with your grant maker. Contact them and tell them exactly what the situation is. They can help you brainstorm solutions and if something needs to be significantly altered from the original plan, they can approve it.

Being honest and using your funder as a partner is always the best solution to dilemmas like these.

4. **<u>Don't miss reporting deadlines</u>**
Most grants (with the exception of some very small, private/foundation grants) have reporting requirements. This means that if and when you get a grant, you will be required to submit weekly, monthly, quarterly, or annual reports demonstrating what activities have taken place, how you've spent grant funds, what type of impact you're observing, and what progress you've made towards achieving benchmarks and goals.

When you're writing a grant request, you may be tempted to agree to any conditions if they will just give you money. Your organization needs it, your boss is counting on you to make it happen, and you have faith that you can satisfy the grant maker one way or another.

Resist that urge! Reporting requirements for grants are

not a suggestion. And they definitely shouldn't be an afterthought. When you decide to apply for a grant, pay special attention to the grant reporting requirements and schedule. Can you gather the data they want? Do you have the manpower to not only gather that data, but also put it into a usable format and make sure it's submitted on time?

If the answer is 'no', then don't submit a proposal. Flaking out on your grant reports can damage the reputation of your nonprofit, its likelihood of getting future grants, and you may even need to repay the grant for which you've missed reports.

Now, stuff does happen, especially when it comes to something like a renovation or new construction project. If you know at some point during the grant period you will not finish the project by the time your report is due, let the funder know this. They have a right to know if your project has experienced a significant setback. If necessary, ask for an extension on your report deadline.

Pro Tip: Having a well thought-out evaluation plan *before* you start applying for grants can not only make you more attractive to grant makers, it can also ensure that you know what types of data gathering and reporting your organization is capable of and willing to do. This is where good program design and evaluation comes in. We covered that in Chapter 3. Don't skip that chapter!

5. **If you are a freelancer or your organization is using a freelance grant writer, payment should never be contingent upon the grant award**

This guideline is surprising for a lot of nonprofits who are unfamiliar with using grant writers. However, it's a common standard that the writer should get paid for their work whether the grant proposal gets funded or not. This is also the standard put forth by both the Grant Professionals Association and the Association of Fundraising Professionals, two very credible professional fundraising organizations in the United States.

Think about it this way: there are a million reasons a great proposal may not get funded. The grant reviewer could be in a bad mood when they read the proposal, they could have changed their funding priorities but not made that clear on the RFP or their website, or they could have pre-emptively chosen which organizations were going to receive awards that year without making that information public. Or, as is often the case, the grant maker received more deserving proposals than they could fund so some fantastic proposals had to be denied out of necessity.

None of those scenarios are a grant writer's fault. And in the meantime, a grant writer has spent untold hours researching the grant opportunity, crafting a well-written proposal, checking facts and plans, collecting data and research to support their case, and editing the final proposal. This work is detailed, time-consuming, and valuable. The grant writer deserves to be paid regardless of the outcome.

If you include consultants in your program budget, they should only be consultants who will help you develop a program, undergo a strategic planning process, or perform some other relevant service directly related to the program. Foundations typically do not like to cover expenses you incurred prior to the grant award, which effectively rules out using your grant to pay a grant writer.

If you are writing grants on a contractual or non-staff basis for nonprofits, ensure that your payment doesn't hinge on the grant being awarded. As Bruce likes to say, if you want to earn commissions, sell Buicks. Otherwise, stick with an hourly rate or a flat fee.

This list is not exhaustive, but we believe if you follow these 5 guidelines you'll manage to avoid 99% of common grant writing pitfalls.

Chapter 11:
When You Should Hire a Freelancer, a Staff Grant Writer, or DIY

If you're an executive director, a board member, or someone who does not particularly enjoy grant writing, at what point should you get an outside grant writer versus doing it yourself?

If you're a new or small organization, you may have no realistic choice but to do it yourself or to find a willing volunteer.

With volunteers, though, your mileage may vary. If you have a consistent, reliable volunteer grant writer, great. However, to get grants, you need to seek them in a systematic fashion, monitor them to make sure they are being used for the stated purpose, and keep funders informed about your progress. It can be difficult to find a volunteer who is: 1) a good enough grant writer to adequately do the job; and 2) committed to this process over an extended period of time.

Many organizations use freelancers. Some retain grant writing consultants like us for an extended period of time. Usually, these organizations are stable, but smaller and do not need a full-time grant writer on staff. Freelancers can be a sound investment even for larger organizations, too, depending on the organization. You don't have to pay benefits to freelancers. You don't have to provide computer equipment or office space for them either, as most consultants work from home.

Another option is to hire a full-time development director who must cover grant writing, special events, and other types of fundraising by themselves. Some fundraising professionals perform well as a jack-of-all-trades. Others do some things better than others. An extroverted fundraiser may find it too isolating to sit in front of a computer for extended periods, as is often necessary with grant writing. Conversely, introverted grant writers like us barely tolerate special events.

Large organizations usually need and have one or more full-time grant writers on staff.

Possible places you can look for a grant writer, or to get recommendations about good grant writers include:

- Local chapters of the Grant Professionals or the Association of Fundraising Professionals;
- Other nonprofit organizations in your area;

- Local foundations; or
- Your local United Way or the arts equivalent in your area

In addition to getting grants, one benefit of finding a good grant writer is it frees up your time and your staff members' time to engage in other tasks, including tasks that directly generate income for your organization.

In Closing

Well, we've taken you as far as we can on this topic for now. A significant part of your learning curve will happen by actually doing the work and learning from your mistakes and successes.

We also hope we've removed some of your fear around grant writing, which is very common. Almost everyone new to grant writing is intimidated by it to one degree or another. It's 100% normal. If you use the information we have given you as a catalyst for action, your fears will gradually subside. No matter how good of a grant writer, you will win some and lose some and, if you do what you said you would, the ones you win will change lives. Grants are a valuable tool for making your community a better place, and we wish you much success in your endeavors!

Appendix

LOGIC MODEL

ORGANIZATION: _____
PROGRAM: _____

ACTIVITY	GOALS	OBJECTIVES	OUTCOMES	RESOURCES	DATA COLLECTION	STAFF ASSIGNED

© PAINTED POST PUBLICATIONS

Logic Model

> **Define the problem or problems to be addressed**

> **What will you do to address these problems?**

> **What is your goal? What do you hope to accomplish?**

Objectives: ↓

Outcomes: ↓

About the Authors

Bruce Ripley has written grant proposals and fundraising letters that have raised over $17 million for nonprofit organizations. He is also a Licensed Clinical Alcohol and Drug Counselor who has authored or co-authored 12 home study courses for counselors and social workers. He lives in Loveland, Ohio.

Ashley Cain has been successfully writing grants for nonprofit organizations for more than a decade, raising millions in funding for programs, projects, and operating costs. She is also the proud owner of Cain Nonprofit Solutions, a consultancy offering grant writing, research, web development, and eTraining services to arts and culture nonprofits. Ashley lives in Fairfield Township, Ohio with her husband and daughter.

www.ingramcontent.com/pod-product-compliance
Lightning Source LLC
Chambersburg PA
CBHW030723220526
45463CB00005B/2153